PALMA CATHEDRAL

The Colorado Prize
David Milofsky, Series Editor

PALMA CATHEDRAL

Michael White

for Terry,

a pleasure meeting you.

Mike

Center for Literary Publishing / University Press of Colorado
Fort Collins

Winner of the 1998 Colorado Prize for Poetry

1 2 3 4 5 02 01 00 99 98

For information about permission to reproduce selections
from this book, write to Permissions, Center for Literary Publishing,
Department of English, Colorado State University, Fort Collins,
Colorado 80523.

Library of Congress Cataloging-in-Publication Data

White, Michael.
Palma cathedral: poems / by Michael White.
p.   cm.
ISBN 0-87081-516-4 (pbk.: alk. paper)
I. Title
PS3573.H47445P34   1998
811'.54—dc21   98–39425
CIP

ACKNOWLEDGMENTS

These poems were first published in the following magazines:

Colorado Review: "Anatomies of Paradise," "Palma Cathedral"

Gulf Coast: "The Death of Turnus"

The Journal: "Ghost Pond," "Her Mother's House," "What I Wanted to Tell You"

New Republic: "Camille Monet Sur Son Lit de Mort," "John Rock," "Pool Hall"

North Carolina Humanities: "The Morning Road"

Paris Review: "Hotel Bar," "The Woman on the Steps of the *Bella Vista* Apts."

Ploughshares: "Bay of Naples," "Port Townsend"

Western Humanities Review: "Here Below," "Promontory Point"

"Camille Monet Sur Son Lit de Mort" was reprinted in *The Best American Poetry of 1994*.

The author gratefully acknowledges The National Endowment for the Arts, The North Carolina Arts Council, Centrum, Yaddo, The Breadloaf Writers' Conference, and The Vermont Studio Center for fellowships received during the completion of this book.

Special thanks are also due to Kathy Fagan, for her patient and insightful encouragement.

CONTENTS

Three things are too wonderful for me,
*   yes, four I cannot understand:*
The way of an eagle in the air,
*   the way of a serpent upon a rock,*
The way of a ship on the high seas,
*   and the way of a man with a maiden.*

— Proverbs 30:18–19

part one

GHOST POND

I stand at the edge of water,
the bandage wrapping my instep
soaked and ravelling off,

like the feverish warmth of sleep.
I could've dreamt a sailboat—
luminous, its newness

come back—fluttering, caught
in the cattails; or my brothers
in a shirr of skate-blades,

clatter of hockey sticks,
and wandered out . . .
                    The town
ends where this path began—

in silent frog-marsh, fencewires
sunk through years of grass—
a mild, wet wilderness.

The shore is slithering rushes.
There is no other side.
And here or there, the surface

shivers to the touch
of no wind I can feel . . .
I know the pond is gone,

the fields are gone, the scar
almost invisible,
but the line of distant oaks

beyond the slopes of pasture
silvers now. I watch
the sharpening light of late March

wash through the river hills,
I stare at the whirling ash
of stars, at everything

so dim—for in these waters
of my first memory,
it is still five a.m.

PORT TOWNSEND

A year after your death, I leaned above
my desk, and listened to gullshrieks rising off
the shoreline I imagined—shapes of driftwood,
glistening sacs of jellyfish, whatever

washes in—page after page of days
misplaced in the leaden interim . . .
                                    One evening,
I felt it before I saw the seam, the tremor
widen—felt the shell-white, shadowed white

roll back across the Sound—
                          And found the stair,
the switchbacks snaking up through hemlocks, tensed
madronas drenched with salt (mist caught in the rusted
wrecks of brambles, smoking in and out

my breath), past sidelong, nearly silent springs
slipped out through raw cuts in the slant rock . . .
Crossing the headland wading wet ferns, lichens
crumbling underfoot, I skirted the derelict,

moss-sunk gun emplacements to the cliffedge
crumbling, undercut—
                    And at that moment—
in that motion, pulse—the cries of warblers
flicked across my shoulder, little flock

of leaf-shapes into the lick of blue. Below,
obsidian sand flats, smooth off-camber rollers . . .
Farther and farther out through rafts of kelp,
an eely coot winked under, coming up

with glints of fish. I watched horizons crumpling
range on range against Mt. Noh, the slow
heart of the lighthouse drifting—drowned—until
the left side of my face froze numb, and I

stepped into the dusk again—its fronds and root-knots,
oblique mists, its echoes of waveshocks even
here—through silvery, insubstantial fir slopes,
traces of cloudsurf far from the sound of water.

HERE BELOW

Time is a horse that runs in the heart . . .
—Wallace Stevens

1

Into the falls of gold and cobalt, Gothic
light unbraiding one sense from another,
I had never seen the human figure
shaped as a radiant grief: an upward smoke—
a downward light—in blank time holding still.

I saw a saint's foot polished by touch or kiss,
the veins completely smoothed away. Whatever
was said about the ceaseless currents of
the faithful, I had no patience; I wanted the perfect
balance of the place, that dizziness

above the Crossing . . .

2

We worked at the bottom of ladders
in a trance, a kind of sleep afflicted
with flooded bilges, sweat, a lavishing
of hours on steamlines, gathering twenty thousand
horses in the mind . . .

But underway—
the moorings cast off, strewing our starry wake—
I dreamt a different ocean out of voices
faintly raining through my headphones
from the bridge: *one-third ahead; full speed . . .*

Theirs was the real sea, the beautiful—
living in crisp whites, constellated brightness
I imagined, setting a course this way
or that across the phosphoring manes of waves,
watching the distant hill-towns disappear—

Our sea could kill us any second. Sunk
in its frigid streams, we sensed it pulsing beyond
the curve of the earth, each breaker racing toward us.
Sometimes, whales glanced off our echoing ribcage;
coral outcrops scoured against our skin . . .

5

Shutting my eyes, I saw the bladed bronze screw
setting its teeth to darkness
                              the rushing cold
of waves beneath us, through us, bearing east.
I couldn't hear through sleeves of static, caught
the great steel throttle wheel by instinct, feel

unconscious, silken—
                        Where we went, winds cried
across the welds of night
                          and in my hands
the shuddering weight of engine came to rest,
the flesh-warm steel of the throttle came to rest
as nothing will ever rest again.

HER MOTHER'S HOUSE

The downwind cries of geese, the shimmering rains
Of birch had fallen away to memory,
But still her cautious slow descent went on,
Unseeing, searching, drowning in the flux
And wash of cancer. There were flurries of panic
Left in her, her mind unfurling, rousing
Itself in fear, in love, her whole frame racked
For air, as all of winter deepened beneath
The cover of morphine. Never again the flesh
Of April, running in northward gusts of fire—
But only Tuesday, Wednesday, Thursday, hours
That fluttered past in threads of dream, her pulse
Thrumming fainter, faster. Finally,
A watery slip of dawn backlit the contours
Of the river hills, and a gathering blueness
Flooded the foyer of her mother's house,
Numbing the civil atmosphere of china
And silver, wrapping original cold around
The curves of the armchairs—
                                        I left her in that light, and walked
Out past the suburbs, holding the warmth of her body
In my hands. December was coming on;
It was close to freezing, the long light breaking
Across the sodden and bird-deserted earth.

THE WOMAN ON THE STEPS
OF THE *BELLA VISTA* APTS.

I followed her gaze past rooftops of tin, fired-clay
and tar, to the lake's far sleights of vision—its gulls
blown sideways and backwards in flight, its islands floating
in their reflections—with lightning rippling the nerves
of distance, and thunderheads massing across the west . . .

And then, for more than an hour, wherever I looked—
the stoplights bleeding like watercolors across
the glass of buildings—she was fixed in the fringe
of sight, her right hand absently clasped in her left:
the woman, the desert, the cloudcover closing off.

Slicked down with a sheen of rain, the streets were strangely
deserted; starlings and litter kept disappearing
through clearings of sky. An occasional passerby
lurched past in the flat relief of a paper cut-out
beneath the heaves of storm. And over and over—

until I was home in the solitude of my dark
apartment—I kept seeing flashes of basin and range
unreeling beneath the first cold stars . . .
                                                        What is it
drawing us out like moths, in shivers of sunlight
sweeping the lake? Why do we give ourselves

to the wind, to vapory helixes of dust,
the longer we live our lives? These are the hours
we recognize our thirst for brokenness,
for lit-shale dusks arrayed on the lavish scale
of our looking, when only the half-healed cut in your palm

can call you back to your body. These are the hours
rain turns the air it dries in iridescent,
lingering like a taste on the tongue, for as long
as this moment lasts, there is no other end
to it, there is no other end in sight

but iron skies, and the irised glow of the moon.

PROMONTORY POINT

Here is a blur
of sunburnt grass, a constant flitter
of goldfinch down the fencewires . . .
                              Deep in the fluent
afternoon, where pelicans smack the lake
like fists, your foot shifts, car drifts, crunching over
salt crust, comes to rest miles past
the last keeled-over, sunbleached farmshack wreckage.
Sometimes flukes of light dissolve
so perfectly in looking, years go by
before the ice floes flame at last, or swarms
of summer stars resolve, caught up in known
treelimbs. You never know you knew it, stone
and river sheen, skin of the world. But could you
take in bones of scrub oak, substance, weight
leached from the white earth? Reefs
of salt mist rise uncertainly across
the lake, and looming softly in and out
the canyon mouths along the Wasatch face,
the faint, archaic shoreline shows itself,
an ocean sunken away beneath its gulls—

A pair of herons, sailing past
like prophecies, see through you, by you, scour
the sedges, feel by wingtip through warm wind.
You've wandered off to watch the flights
of geese that follow the far shore:
rapid, easeful, bunching or trailing back,
each wingflick tangled and bound. Beyond
these startled dashes—gull cries, tongues of glare—
beyond the smokelike downward swirl of vultures
figured there, all detail burns off under
scaffoldings of heat. Tonight, a grassfire
wicks through sleep, transparent, pouring out . . .
But now you track your footprints back, as if
you had all day. O traveler, something plays
such tricks, the spirit rushing, falls back,
still believing it could pass untouched,
like the shadows of clouds or of birds.

HOTEL BAR
for Larry Levis (1946–1996)

This was the year drought autumn never ended.
Rivers couldn't float their barges, prairies
burned in a sulphurous caul, dead blossoms and clots

of cloud hung bloodshot, strung out over the west
horizon . . . I remember headlights lost in
miles of afternoon, peninsulas

of dustpall rolling off the failed fields, glare-swept
freeways sliding into a waning city
of streetlamps and smokestacks and billboards and Baptist spires.

And this was the year they renovated, gutted
wholesale blocks of downtown—brickheaps and tangled
fire escapes—and staked out naked saplings

next to the rubble. Not that it mattered much
to me. The Cheers was always the same inside—
its gestures left unfinished, monologues

that looped back over and over. Always the same
few regulars just getting warmed up—forearms
pressed against the marble bartop—trembling,

painful to look at. Even when I didn't want to
I could hear their money singing, feel the ice
in the pits of their stomachs, each one slipping piecemeal

through stale arabesques of smoke. And soon the evening
carhorns and streetcries, creak of the canvas awning
outside . . . Soon, the slats of soiled light pouring

into their ruined faces, irises
lit brilliant as the sunstruck liquors racked
in tiers behind me. In the meantime—scarred hills

risen half-drowned at the ends of streets—
I'd watch each stranger passing, shrieks of steampipes
pulsing toward the suites of another world . . .

Before long then, the blood of memory thinned.

And I don't know what drew them there, what pinned
them—rummaging the false leads of their lives

for scattered crumbs of jokes or come-ons—but
I know how it feels when language comes back, crust
and pith you tear with your teeth. I know how it feels

so far from God, the distance you must travel
through tapped out in alphabets of fire.
It's like driving some floodplain two-lane south

through the boredom of alfalfa fields at night—
when you think of nothing, till some half-real bridge
of your childhood arcs against alluvial darkness—

It's like crossing with one thrust of the mind—
the river's silver spilt beneath—when girders
flick past and immaculate, moonlit islands

rip you open, when you cup the Present
in both hands, and lift it to your lips.

ANATOMIES OF PARADISE

1

Wordless, half-starved, drunk with sun, we stared
through weltering depths of dustflicks, spinning beneath
the tarred ties—stared at the shrunken, acid-green
creekbed of this world, sunk between stone pilings.

This was the Devil's Backbone bridge, wind-trembled
filagree of rust and rotten timber.
This was the seething August south of town,
its fevers of bindweed lapping the foot of quartz cliffs . . .

Now I wish I remembered more than the outlines of ridges
of cedars staggering toward us, of faint roads trickling
through ravaged orchards, and stubborn ghosts
of barns. I wish I remembered more than the motion

of scrabbling through willow-scrub out of this picture,
into the upper reaches of hardwoods, and into
the gold-panelled swampoak dusk. But nothing could hold
our attention for long then, climbing through cobweb, through hummocks

of alder (where you were the consciousness behind me, quick
as the leaf-snap back in my mind); through the wreckage
of deadfall, sumac and wildrose, into the light-filled
weedfields beyond. And nothing could touch us, sleeping

or waking or dangling our legs across the cliff-ledge;
watching the shadow-line approaching—sweeping
the floodlands, edge to edge—each milelong trough
of wind stilled in its medium of ochre

all the rest of our lives. The rest of our lives
we'll watch the hourslant break up, blaze, an ingot
incandescing on the lip of limestone
outcrop—then not even that . . .
                                        Years later

(caught in the image-drift of a lungful of smoke
in one neighborhood dive or another),
                                        this was the moment
I would disappear into, this hour,
this air, this miscellaneous rapture of

minutiae, crickets and treefrogs. Here's the motion
I'd imagine: stepping light, slipping between
slack fencestrands (barbed wire burned deep into our hands),
or tearing new paths through the sloughs of canebrake, back

to the creek again . . . These shadows and gravel and restless
shallows stumbling through themselves,
these ghostly minnow-flickerings through sheets
of evening. Out of the undercut pools, smallmouths

striking at water-skaters; hulls of turtles
drifting beneath the backswept willows . . . Swallows
skim the algal afterglow, the night's
one-hearted, ravening cry repeats, repeats

and we press through it, keeping what we claw
for ourselves (the horse burrs caught in the fray of our cutoffs),
crawling through actual briars and vine-snarl,
plunging headlong into the dark of water.

2

Hundreds of suns collected in facades
of tense and bricked-in silence—sepia leached
by halftones, halfnotes—now the town floats hazebound

toward the end of summer. Suburbs wash
through night's low hills like blue-white aisles of embers . . .
How can we rest, when loose, continuous chords

of scent well out of the hedged darkness
of good neighborhoods? How could we lie still—stay still—
our knuckles black with newsprint, in our skulls

the systole, diastole of footsteps? Soon
the great, shambling streetsweeper casts its morose,
yellow uproar through the sleep of parked

cars and deep anchored oaks; and all night, over
the moonblind vacancies and slate roofs of
our common hearts, the oldtown coalstack towers,

its watery smokestream sketched across fixed reefs
of silt and silver . . .

These are the saturate, star-stilled nights
limb-lightness sets in, like an ingrained ache

of bone or nerve-net drawn back to its limestone
damp. And these are the paths of least resistance—
currents of root-buckled sidewalks, flights

of stone stairs reeling nowhere, memories
of railing rippling through our fingers . . . Out here,
half asleep ourselves, we catch the drift

of others' dreams, confuse the smell of girls
we love with luminous rosebeds, rows of headstones
filing through the ashen first light. Look

across the railyard laid in rust—untouched,
anonymous—at panes of dayfall shattered
among the loading docks and warehouse alleys:

there is our burnt-out roofscape, unchanged—peeling
billboards, ads dissolved—the sun's dull white edge
struggling through the smoke and smudge of harvest.

part two

POOL HALL

By the time I was 28, the evening shift
at Booche's seemed like all I had ever known,
especially after the day crowd drifted home

and left me watching the shallow cast of sunlight
inching down the white formica bartop—
shoals of cigarette smoke in back, and the clack

of eightball. As for the regulars who held on,
clinging to some shore of their creation:
better to keep quiet, better to let them cling,

the purgatorial fires of Happy Hour
suffusing one side of their faces . . . It was
easy to see there was no turning back,

oblivion blooming in the mirror's waters . . .
Staring out at the rows of glarestruck storefronts—
powerlines and smokestacks washed in gold—

I thought it was perfect. I thought I'd be there forever,
tending that lull, waiting on the drowned . . .
For I knew every cocktail recipe,

the secret physics of bankshots, and could read
the tension smouldering through the slag of dusk,
the ashen ache of exposed riverbanks

that set our teeth on edge. Night after night
I'd pour one-handed, one eye on the street—
as cloudreefs burned incarnadine through gaps

in the stunned skyline. Sometimes, no one spoke
for hours—their bodies rocking a little, fixed
on glints and knots of light in the stacked glassware—

rapture flooding through soldered nerves . . . They'd slide
their empties towards me, each soul boarded up
but conscious of these seconds ticking, freeways

droning just beyond the outskirts of
this view—these blank marquees and sidewalk trees,
this smoky blush of plate-glass—as each green

and swallow-crossed dusk deepened, and slipped away.

WHAT I WANTED TO TELL YOU

for Rebecca Lee

couldn't wait, and I kept taking the steps
    to your beachhouse three at a time in my mind, but
the truth is, I was caught in traffic back
    in Forest Hills. Before I knew what hit me—

what the slowdown and clanging hysteria meant—the tandem
    diesels lumbered past, all decibels
and oilsmoke, and then maybe a hundred coalcars
    and flatcars slid through the fogged dusk. I admit

I loved the spectacle, the patience of joggers
    and leashed dogs—even the starlings swirling up
from the blossomy lungs of the live oaks—and I wanted
    to step out, rush into that magnitude

the way my mind does sometimes, going for broke,
    not letting go . . . But I stayed firmly put
instead, and slipping into neutral, read
    the boxcars' open secrets: *Big Blue, Norfolk*

& Western scrolling through the neighborhood—
    where mansions shuddered in their berths, where April
sulked and lost its grip, where in the wrack
    of body heat, the agony of steel

on steel, I spoke to you like this.

SIREN

All night, lashed to the mast of dream, it seemed
the flowering trees—azaleas drunk on ether—
even the glossy knives of the magnolias

shivered in the least breeze of your voice.
In fact, as I found out later—flailing through
vague densities of indigo (my body

knotted in twists of sheets, the ceiling fanblades
all that swirled between me and the milky
fiords of constellations)—this was true.

But in the meantime, what could I do? Midnight's
spidery machinery spread across
the coastal plain; I couldn't move, or call

your name. I saw myself asleep there—flayed
and witless—while outside, a surf of whiteness
broke, erupting through black loam, black bark.

I can't recount what happened next, or how
it was I stepped out, slipped out blind into
a startling night ablaze with text, the earth's

sap wicking up through its lush rhetoric
of heart and xylem.
                          That's when I started walking—
drifting along moon-drizzled sidewalks—past

identical lawns, the thoughtless symmetries
of streets, whole neighborhoods where nothing stirred
except a couple of porch dogs cocked their heads.

My limbs burned with an unbelievable lightness—
landscape after landscape rolling past—
and even the shoulders of roads seemed made for me.

I remember wandering through the spiel of mourning
doves just winding up—the uniform dark
of pine marsh broken here and there by steely

glimpses of tidal creeks—and here and there,

my mind came unhinged, hungering over the tassels
of reeds, and of saltgrasses leaning toward the sea . . .

And, crossing the drawbridge—standing on the seam—
I stared down into an estuarine calm, the waterway's
mute rows of fishing boats lined up like souls . . .

And all I remember after that is haze,
and the violet streaks of rapture. This was after
I passed through dunes (the night-soothed sand so soft,

so smooth), and came to the leading edge of things—
illegible scrawls of sandcrabs all around me,
caches of clamshells and mussels. Facing the breakers

pounding in against it, Crystal Pier
braced on its forelegs, flexing its long spine . . .
The city slept behind me. Nothing stirred

except the backwash seething at my feet—
the ore of cirrus far offshore, brushed up
in loose processions over the Sargasso . . .

Suddenly, without thinking, I was running
full stride into the dull-slate seas—the weight
of whitecaps cutting me off at the knees—and kept on

lunging and stumbling sidelong into the crumpling
shock of the surf—which gathered head and crushed me
over and over, until I had crossed the shoals.

It took a long time. Mostly, I half-walked, half-swam—
letting the tide-rip carry me farther and farther
beyond the inlet mouth, the end of the island

gradually shifting north . . .
                              By then I was free,
backstroking effortlessly over the windless
glassgreen swells: flotillas of jellyfish;

the shadows of sandsharks moving deep beneath me;
pelicans winging past in twos or threes . . .
By then I could see the broader view of condos

bleached the color of sand, the dingy beach-towns

of America. I spread my arms wide,
kicked my feet, and looked back at my life

as everything—the pier, the empty strand,
the delicate ephemerae of dunefields—
even the smoky overcast above

the mainland disappeared across the broken
water—
          and, instead of turning back
toward shore (the body of Gulf Stream warm and clear,

the seafloor sloping away below), I woke.

JOHN ROCK

for Dan Noland

Fingerlings pocked the surface from beneath
where mossed logs crossed the creek, a luminous shock
of green suffusing the birches . . .
       Maybe an hour
passed like that, deep in the understory of ferns,
and then the path forked: switchback after switchback

worked upslope in earnest, into the static
body of overcast, coves of the Fraser firs.
The rest of the day, through talus, rockslide, and snowmelt
violets (like small explosions of blood in my brain),
I climbed through the earliest drafts of March, and though

I couldn't make out much in the matte-white fogswell
washing over the Cat Gap when I crossed—
when the trail eased through the ridgecrest scrub-oaks, thickets
of rhododendron, onto the lichened skull
of John Rock—I knew suddenly where I was.

I knew where I was because I'd studied the contours,
elevations; I'd considered Pisgah
ridge by ridge—imagining the climb,
the cold topographies I'd learned by heart,
long views across the Piedmont and the plain.

But there was nothing there: I looked out on
that surface of mercurial calm—the level
cloudmass islanding the overlook—
and far beyond, vast plateaus, faultlines, but
no other view, as far as I could see . . .

No seaboard, mind of God, no "deep and gloomy
breathing-place" a half mile off, and nothing
beneath me but the faintly venous blue
rifts in the flesh of weather, whiter cirrus
banked up over interiors of ash.

And in that gaze—that instant—I shrank back,
and started jogging down the long way back
through the mist and drizzle of coniferous darkness;
I could already feel the switchbacks buckling,
the entire mountainside unfolding in

slow motion . . .

> Then, a bit of light at the end
> of the loop, my car parked next to a silted creek
> in the sweet, deciduous landscape of the living.

THE MORNING ROAD

1

Another afternoon slips off
in feints of rain, in streams of taillights
flickering through the very currents
memory is composed of,

a slow dusk buckling upon itself.
Now, banking far out over the lake,
the wings of an airplane frozen in glare,
the sun's coin glazing the windshields of cars,

the city gathering in half sleep out of
slag hills, cliffs of cirrus, sweep
of lights and shadows on the landscape,
skies revisiting the skies.

These flushes of copper green, for instance—
ringing with shouts of children—come
from an evening walk eight years ago,
the end of summer filling the ends

of streets—Hedges were lying low,
gardens were settling in their sweet glooms,
rooms lighting here or there in houses
we imagined living in—

2

But even these half-dreamt dusks wear down
in scattered stars, as struck sparks arc
through silences and distances
as vast as heaven. Here, again,

a storm of light motes rushes the headlights—
lashes the dead-beat eye in waves—
as we drove your old Dodge full out into
the dark of another life. It was midnight,

the Rockies, December of the year
before. We raced through flailing luffs
of snow, the passes closing off
behind us. Sudden glimpses of sheer

drop-offs loomed beside us and vanished,
with lone peaks trailing silvery spumes
in fragmentary vistas. Soon
we couldn't have known how we kept on

through the blindness spinning against us, into
a wind-cleared wilderness of stars,
subzero clarities, the car
rising and falling dreamlike over

the buried highway. I glanced at your face
in the faint dash-glow, our snowblank minds
plummeting on through walls of wind,
the steering wheel numb in my hands.

3

What was it like, that light-chinked porch
nailed onto the end of sunrise or sunset,
stilted beneath where the mountainside
sloped off? All I know is the arch

of my foot still wraps around the feel
of the rough-adzed steps that tumbled down
from the cabin to the trail. I'd known
you a month, that morning, and thought it was over.

Ahead of me, the forest floor
was a sunken hush of sego lilies;
behind, in the rush of snowmelt and downdraft,
the house stood stationed in the air

where I had left you coming to
and drifting off, the canvas blind
of the screendoor wafting out in wind.
Something was rooting me to that spot—

the trace of last night's pine smoke, thread
of mist in the aspen, squabble of magpie?
It felt remembered even then,
as I walked down the morning road.

THE DEATH OF TURNUS

Traytor, dost thou, dost thou to Grace pretend,
Clad as thou art, in Trophees of my Friend?
                              —Dryden's *Aeneid*

1

Far on the outskirts Turnus watched in dread
as firebrands rained into the wounded city
rooftops falling in in sheets of flame . . .

He took a step . . . He broke out in a dead run
toward the town, flying through undergrowth
without pain or effort, like a ghost

down paths of its childhood. Approaching the Trojan lines
that ringed Laurentum, scattered stragglers stared
at him in wonder: without breaking stride

he cut through rank on rank of troops drawn up
in earshot of the front, their earthworks—pitchfires—
horses shivering in the dew-drenched shade . . .

He ran through the roaring of his own blood, and there
in the midst of the siege itself, smoke drifting over
the cleared ground—singing of arrows—thudding hooves

of the cavalry in sorties, called him out

2

Beneath an eerie mingling of Latins and Trojans,
women thronging the ramparts, craning to see
Aeneas himself in gold and crimson—awed
by the pine-tree spear, and the spectacle of the shield—

There far below, two figures fumed in glare
closed hand to hand, as Turnus lunged for blood—
flaring up at full height, lashing out—
the shield at first shock shattering his blade—

and ran again
on dream-legs drained of sense, stared at the broken
hilt he still held hemmed-in circling treading
water blankness lostness stride for stride

his life poured out like water. He heard Aeneas
gasping for air, and the distant cries of friends—
each footfall   breath   all happening again
as he'd imagined it. He called to his friends

for his own sword, their faces blank as the walls
that shadowed him. Sleepwalker-slow beneath
the yoke of armor, raving
five times around that tract of trampled earth,

at last he spotted a huge stone, wrenched it loose
in one swoop, staggered beneath its mass
a little way, and hurled it against Aeneas—
but as he bent and gathered himself, his knees

gave out, and the boulder, conjured there against
the blue of dream, fell short at the other's feet.
And everyone watched what had been written happen
as Aeneas let it fly with all his might;

everyone listened with one ear to the hymn
of the hurtling spear, the sharp report of impact
punching through bronze armor. One cry swept
the crowd of Rutulians, one cry shouted back

from oaktrees swayed in wind like anchored men-
o'-war, as Turnus reeled and crumpled on
his gored leg, looking for all the world like someone
losing his balance on the ocean.

3

Still in sight of pastures drowsed with bees,
ordinariness he was the issue of,

Turnus gouged the dust he lay in, mind
clouded but coming to. He propped himself

on one arm, drinking in the air of heaven,
images of leaffire falling loose—

and skittish flames like torn sails blown from mast
to mast   from hull to hull of the Trojan fleet

its rigging and moorings melted off like cobwebs—
as if for him alone   an apparition

taking form he had no words for—one
by one ships shuddered and swam off   cutting the waves

together   homing seaward like a school
of dolphins
                    What bore them back at last was time

in dusk of sawshriek   clatter of chain and cartwheel
when pyres of cargoed numberless and nameless

cast off on Laurentum plain.
                                    Now all light
blazed across Aeneas' breastplate: Turnus,

king of the humming weeds, raised his right hand
in ritual: *Lavinia is your bride,*

he said, *But go no further out of hatred.*
And these words moved Aeneas

so much that who he saw, who prayed for his life
was Pallas, wearing the swordbelt Turnus had stripped

from him, and in a flinch of rage he called
for *Pallas   Pallas*   roaring out the echoed

syllables across the spilled gold ridges
of riffling heat, his swordthrust driven home

through cuirass and the cage of bone within.

"CAMILLE MONET SUR SON LIT DE MORT"

for Jackie

1

Not a picturing. Unclosing landscape
Of disorder: unreadable beneath
The furor of paint, a purely human image
Swims through the scumbled surface of unbeing,
The eyebrows lost in absence. The bluish curve
Of her faint, drawn lips; the bluish glint of her teeth.
Cascading, matted through the loose folds of
Her shroud, the momentary hues of death
Sweep out in nameless energies into
The slippery nuances of reverie:
Blunted silvers, rose and gold dragged clear
Across the flow of canvas. Holding a handful
Of withered violets clutched in an unseen hand.

2

When forty years had passed—in his garden
Slashing stroke by stroke into the dark
Of cataract—he still held one reproach
Against himself. He said: "Nothing is
More natural than the urge to record one last
Image of a person departing this life. . . ."
But nothing could blur the stabbing, recurrent
Memory of his eye as it "searched for
The arrangement of color gradations that death was imposing
On her motionless face. Blue, yellow, gray,
Who knows what else? That was the point I had reached."
It was the last in the series of Camilles—
La femme with the parasol, or in the green
Silk dress; *au bord de l'eau* or *au jardin*—
But this time she has slipped past, into the lighted
Immaterial atmosphere of the bedclothes,
Floating beyond the fine inflections of pain.
This time she slips beyond his streaming skeins
Of paint, her faintly transfixed smile of death
Like a merely spectral scrawl in space, as if,
In the dawn's soft loosening, he tried to wake,
And could not see, and reached for a vanishing dream.

3

Like a coda to the years you clawed death back,
You tried to die four days before you could—
But then found the slim way through. Unsustaining,
Unsustained, your ravished heart sped on
Four days past air and water, breath and blood,
Your face exhausted, drawn, magnificent.
In the moments after, each of us gazed at you
With a nearly unearthly hunger. Frozen blue
In the predawn sky, the lawns of the cul-de-sac
Were framed by the bedside window, and I could see
The stars above, sharp flicks of stars that shimmered
As if in chills of wind. As gently as
I could, I lay beside you, took your hand,
And let your warmth pass slowly into me.

BAY OF NAPLES

The city is still the same handful of glances,
glimpses of alleyways like wounds laid open,
balconies of laundry drying, names of streets
unfolding in the smells of fishscale, kelp,
and poverty . . .
                Across Fleet Landing, sheets
of blind-white glare seethe off the spires and stairflights
through me, through my sea-pitched, sea-numb body,
toward the sea. I'd like to drink myself
civilian, thread my way through troughs of dusk,
past cafe tables set immaculate
beside some nondescript, scummed-over fountain,
April's glassy strata spinning itself
apart above Vesuvius—
                  but in
this rivering air of angels, algae, waves
of language rolling through me, I can't tell
how much I've spent, or anything I've heard . . .
Arriving here lightheaded in the shadow
of Castel Nuovo, reeling a bit
on solid rock, I am a memory
the hookers and gypsies sing to,
passing through the gates into the city.

ONE HUNDRED MILES

1

We lived on catwalks built around what counted.
Standing in one place, I could peer through the pane
of glazed, steam-clouded plexiglass, and see his face
in a wavering dusk of lit fires, roaring mass
of the boilers, crouching perfectly pale and calm

beneath a vent duct. Waiting for a sign,
I'd suddenly let loose with a blur of throttles—
wordless in the sulphurous dimness seven decks
beneath the surface—every arterial tremor
held in the hissing air between our eyes.

But the violent boil of water off the screw
I'd have to imagine, sunlight curling over
and over, feathering the Gulf Stream wake . . .
I'd have to imagine whatever it was
we fired at with the forward guns, shock shuddering

the deckplates, ringing through steel-conscious souls . . .
I'd have to imagine blue sky by the lungful,
dolphins or landfall . . .
                              Meanwhile, the hull rocks hard
in breaking seas, as I open the logbook, translate
thousands of gallons of fuel oil, steam, and salt

and set them down as so many rpm—

2

Coming suddenly on swerves of river,
cooling whiffs of sassafras, the road
dips down, mist swirls materialize as solid
limestone shelving over water—glaze
of shallows, trestles sewn of glass—and then

unspools straight up the other side. It seems
like yesterday—these fog-capped cowponds, sagging,
sun-slashed barns, deep hayfields sparked with fireflies—
wending toward the smoky afterglow
I somehow connect with a town. How often

I have walked here, stared back deer in waves of aster,
truck fumes welling through the exhausted edges
of August. This time I am twenty-one,
light-headed, AWOL, everything I've learned
dismantled wheel by wheel in New Orleans or Norfolk . . .

All I see lies drowned in leaffall, fires,
foundations sunk in a country of blackberry canes,
the tracks long taken up, even the grade
slipped syllable by syllable downstream.
But I am less than a hundred miles from home,

a rubble of houselights quickly sketched, where you
are still alive. It feels like yesterday,
these starlings scattering ridge to ridge, this shrill
of gnats near ditches . . .
                              And breath comes easier now
in the evening coolness—glimpses of huddled lightning

above a day I haven't imagined yet . . .

part three

PALMA CATHEDRAL

The island cathedral of Palma de Mallorca, Spain, nicknamed "La Seu" by the Mallorcans, reaches the highest pitch in the line of Catalan hall-churches. The tourist, often arriving from Barcelona, the nearest Peninsular city, might naturally draw mental comparisons between the two seaport cathedrals, especially since Barcelona's softly sculptured interior is extraordinarily dim, while Palma is the only luminous sanctuary in the Levant, and perhaps the finest achievement in light of the Gothic world. As one enters Barcelona, the sepulchral murk gives an immediate physical chill; it takes several minutes for the eye to become accustomed to the dark. Then the remote blackness yields dramatically to exquisite gradations of burnt umber and sea-floor green, pierced at far intervals by a jeweled light from above. The material fabric of Palma, on the other hand, is everywhere infused with a deliberate antithesis, a severe and single-minded focus on the qualities of the Balearic sun. It is usually thought to have been the master Jaime Fabre, called to Barcelona from Palma in 1317, who was largely responsible for both.

1

But for the eyes of unfaith, for this one
Who stepped from equatorial noon into
This voluted shell—into the strong sun sloped
Through numinous diffusions of softer white—
It was to step from darkness into the light.
Here he saw nothing; he couldn't get used to the scale.
The great jeweled rose mooned high in the clifflike west,
Pouring in a delirium of blazing
Blue and crimson; while, along the chiseled
Surfaces, deep in the traceried chapels
And smoky dependencies, shadows were felt
As folds in the light, tints lacking a definite source.

2

Climbing the steps of the Placa de Cort, he'd noticed
A certain numbness in his step; he felt it again
When he counted his first pesetas out to the guard;
Now his sea-legs wouldn't quite work. It was as if
He could sense the depth and weight of the bedrock the pavement
Rests on in each individual nerve,
As his stiff, spit-polished dress-leather shoes
Scuffed forward awkwardly across the vast
Reverberant floor of the nave—and that sound, with its painful
Reproach, froze him slowly where he stood;
He could feel the individual veins in his neck;
The individual pulse of the blood enthralled:

For there was Time held in a grace of sense,
In a forest of white stone pillars, the slenderest, plainest,
Octagonal columns in Christendom, which rose
On one breath through this bright hull of the mind,
Through rays of light let in at the lateral bays
As if through random cloud-rifts, and did not end
At their limits, but, capital-less and flaring like palms,
They arced in light momentum all directions
Into the haze of height.
                              He didn't know
How to look at it, this fiery heart
Of luminosity, vault after vault
Thrown high and effortless as flame, the image
Still unfolding as he took it in.
Within the ghostliest inferences of hearing,
As if a memory softly kept recurring
To him, a steady stressless murmur of
The Mass came floating from the distant cloisters
Behind the altar, and the aftertones
Of prayer still crept along the stone as slowly
As the warm white splay of light explored the place
Contrived by Fabre for it—which is what that
High room exists to do.
                              He moved, and felt
Exhausted by his body's weight, but he saw
Each capturable hue in the sun struck through
The lens of fenestration, through the steep
Topographies of memory: densely whorled
With gold and candle-smoke, each sunshaft made
Its slow traverse of its allotted length

Of marble. And each step woke within him some
Keen incorporeal separate sight that marked
The tiny observer—free of earthly claims,
With no idea yet of what his life would be—
As he scuttled on through the watery-pale arcaded
Chamber of coral light as it drifts at sea.

3

He passed vaguely thus toward the *retablo mayor*,
Toward Gaudi's raveling wrought-iron fantasy
Suspended in mid-air above the altar.
Walking unconscious, in the contemplation
One accords to scenery in a dream;
Approaching, pausing, then, as gravely, passing
From this thought into a cavernous portal,
Through waves of fire-ribbed vaults set in the gradually
Lightening vermeil tones of their own shade . . .
And out through the mouth of Puerta del Mirador,
Onto the vast and vacant promenade
Of the Great Porch, where darkness was pooled beneath
The massing of counterfort and buttress. Built
On the edge of the Odyssey's world, railed like a ship,
It faced a sea as dense as melted glass,
An azure almost more than the eye could stand.
Hundreds of feet above, each white stone wing
Spanned a field of flawlessly cold-blue sky—
The same lunar blue of the rose within.
But he was merely aware of wanting a smoke,
And a vague desire to shake off the dream that held him,
To realize where he was . . .
                              Everything
In the world was blue or white; even the birds
Were white and specter-like, their movements heavy
And slow. And slowly, he began to see
How things were here, how the monotony
Of sun had singed the fawn-colored hills
To the very rock, so that nothing could grow but the snowlike
Tufts of almonds and olives; where lives were lived
In relief, defined against the glass-sharp sky
As clear as the outlines of houses or La Seu.
It was a kind of doubled trance: beneath
The tiers of greater and lesser buttresses,
The slim grace of the lancets, he was half present
In a calligraphy of piers and vaults,
Or else it was the structure of ideas
Itself—its music of preconscious stone—
That haunted the conscious light.

4

Into this fullness,
Furthest mirage of Europe, the bells of the battered
Romanesque tower began to strike the hour,
In pure, explosive, measured notes that spread
Like cannon-shot across the calm expanse
Of harbor, past the curved arms of its pilings
That reached out into nothingness—where the blue
Wall of the sky fell short of the deeper turquoise
Light of the sea—and where his toylike ship lay moored,
With its fresh coat of gray, its foolish and gay
Little flags . . . But he didn't recognize it.

5

Some visitors think that the crooked little streets
Of the island towns, with their startling flights of stairs
And deserted plazas, wind as they do in defense
From the unrelenting heat and glare. But at night,
When you look for the few stars you know in that knife-edged air—
Unfiltered, undimmed by damp or the breath of cities—
When you cannot tell them apart in that tenfold clutter
Of mingled and faint-blue figures of the sky;
In the watery-white pulsating spirals of galaxies;
In the brief, deliberate flame of the long-tailed comets;
Then even you may long for a close, cramped roofline,
And for streets that cower and writhe.

6

In pictures, you can see the Inner City
Radiating upward and outward through
Ring upon ring of Saracen parapets,
Through archways and cobbled paths that zigzag at memories
Of bastions dismantled for eight hundred years . . .
And it gradually fades in the narrowing later accretions;
In the character of embattlement immersed
Through the grain of the quarried rock; in the martial rhymes
Of chimney and castellated garden gate;
But then blooms again in the apogees of final
Escarpments—vantage points for cannon and camera—
And dies off in the outskirt hills, in the relic
Backdrop of Palma's postcard almond blossoms.

7

Frozen in memory, the carcasses
Of pigs have been taken down from the butchers' doorways.
A pair of priests come walking in some great hurry,
Ducking their heads against a breeze which only
Sharpens the stagnant smell of brine. Bits
Of flowers or paper flutter beneath his feet,
As he follows flowing schemes of colonnade
And shadow—whispers flickering through the stone
As walls exhale, in subtle ticks and tremors,
The warmth of sun they have absorbed all day.
Hugging the curves of precincts marching down
To the sea, the sacramental streetlamps burn
With a bluish flame . . . Farther along the shore,
Punctuating the inky, indefinite bulk
Of hillsides crowned with a skillfully spotlit spire
Or cross, the wandering lights of torches zigzag
Back and forth . . . Blue dusk, nightfall, deep blue night.

8

A bloody alley scuffle: seeing *him*,
Two figures break off savagely kicking a third
Slumped shape . . . Marines, they vanish lightly. The victim,
Rising in brilliant terror, without a word
Spits darkness into the dark, and flees. "Is it late
Enough for this already?" he wonders, sliding
His nightstick back in its loop. Over the water,
White and lucent as shell, La Seu in floodlights
Blazes. Voices, smoke, from a near café:
Out through its glow steps the moment's platinum whore,
Muscled and naked beneath her silver lamé
Miniskirt. Another, like her, joins her,
And they coo like doves at him, in Minorcan
Or Moroccan . . . *The sweet hour coming on.*

9

There is a brooding hesitation, a barely
Discernible uncertainty, in the way
The bay calms momently, then writhes across
In quick and scriptlike shivers, the quayside water

Dark as the Atlantic. He is alone
On the starboard bridge, a plume of steam off his coffee;
In the time it takes his eye to track a gull
Winging its way inland, low, just tipping

The waves as it crosses the riffling lane of light,
The ship casts off, in a voluble muted hush,
Past handfuls of homing gulls and cormorants.
All week, beneath the violent blue of space,

The ocean burned with a false light of its own,
A dubiously brilliant ultramarine; all week,
In this harborage of yachts, the gray ship rusted,
Homely, cargoless, and listing a little,

A source of familial embarrassment to her sailors.
Now, far-distant figures of virga feather
Downward to nothingness, and the whole hull brims
With purpose, as its clean prow scissors the hills

Of the sea that meet them at the deepwater buoy.
Lulled half asleep by the slow return from land,
He dimly hears the blade of the rudder groan
Like an iron door, and braces himself by instinct

Against the turn, against the head-on force
Of the storm, as they heel over into it,
The wing of the bridge inclined to the fire-gapped sky.
He holds on with one hand, through a roll so deep

And ponderous, the blackened, torn-off line
Of the horizon cants up crazily
Ahead; the endless churning sprawl of their wake
Curls scintillant astern. And soon, to starboard,

Palma's filagree of spires and steeples,
Its stucco sidestreets and modern beach resorts
Come into view like tableaux looming dully
Through discordant wastes of thought,

Half-glimpses sliding away beyond recall;
As, into the dome-and-statuary skyline,
Into the idle windings of alleyways,
A bluish inchoate winter wanders in

With its mists of nicotine and musk.
                                              The ship
Runs coastwise into the will of the world, whitecaps
Smashing across her bows, cataracts
Of ocean-water pouring over every

Ledge and ladder, while, in the foredeck clutter
Of boom and landing boat, through cutting winds
Raked out of the massed-up west, two deckhands
Are stowing or lashing something down—small blots

Against the drench of the sky. He can hardly see them,
But he knows exactly who they are. He knows
This scene, the strangely undefined hour of the day;
This grainy, silvered light; the streaks of spray

That stream straight off the breakers; he knows this way
Of looking back at things; the singsong of
The hull, its curves, its shape of humanness
Forever plunging on through darkness; and that

The following dawn will find them in the Straits,
The presence of Gibraltar sliding past,
Where, with a sudden hiss like rain through trees,
The flying fish shoot up from wave to wave.

Sliding upon the water, amorphous wraiths
Keep barring his line of sight, but the city still
Shows through in parts beneath the cold rawness
Of a broken dawn. The docks to the left; the cliffs
Of tourist resorts to the right—all curiously blank,
But filled, he knows, with exhausted English and Germans.
Up in the hill-town proper, the sunburned ones
Who live here are also dead to this world. Chains
Of the faint, unfocused blooms of streetlamps hover
Behind the fog-banks; still, through intimate breaks
Above, some blinking neon hotel signs
Cling by a thread to the night. One clear gap drifts
Until, swaying precipitously in
The wind, the date-palms of the Parc du Mar
Rise from a soft cascade of calla lilies;
A moment later they submerse again,
Their feathery fronds the last to vanish. Here,
A length of rich boutiques along the Rambla;
There, an enormous dockside crane looms out
Of a solid cloud-slope like a stranded crab.
Caught in an undertow of sixteen years,
Each image severed, isolated in
Its foreignness, each indicating forms
The day might take . . .
                                        Soon the heaps of mussels,
Black as India-ink, and the limp, wet roots
Of squid will be spilled out on beds of ice
In the sidewalk cafés, and they will never look
More real than this; the lyric fancy of
The hilltop castles will never appear more real.
Now all of Palma has disappeared, absorbed
Beneath the shifts of mist, and only La Seu
Herself is left. Made to be seen from the sea,
She seems to be sculpted weightless from the water;
Her idiom, her upward unity
Of stone, slips into a havoc of forgetting.
Now the white advance of cloud consumes
The petal-like articulation of
The buttresses, and now the nave, for all
Its immensities of shapen light,
Founders before his eyes. This is the instant
The great west end sinks into the north of distance,

Into the seethe and trouble of the sea,
With its rose, and the tranquil caves of its triple doors,
But the retinal aftereffects of its tower ghost on
Through reaches of fog, until even that is gone.

Souls beyond selfhood caught
know, not knowing, there:
burst the mind's barrier.

—St. John of the Cross, "Deep Rapture," ll. 50–52
(Tr.: John Frederick Nims)

. . . yet even then
In that distraction and intense desire
I said unto the life which I had lived,
Where art thou? . . .

—William Wordsworth, *The Prelude* (1805), XIII, ll. 372–75